? COMMUNITY · CONNECTIONS

WHAT DOES IT DO?
CEMENT MIXER

BY GAETANO CAPICI

Published in the United States of America by Cherry Lake Publishing
Ann Arbor, Michigan
www.cherrylakepublishing.com

Content Adviser: Louis Teel, Professor of Heavy Equipment, Central Arizona College
Reading Adviser: Cecilia Minden-Cupp, PhD, Literacy Consultant

Photo Credits: Cover and page 1, ©iStockphoto.com/kozmoat98; page 5, ©airphoto.gr/
Shutterstock, Inc.; page 7, ©iStockphoto.com/dlewis33; page 9, ©iStockphoto.com/
BanksPhotos; page 11, ©Robert Kyllo/Shutterstock, Inc.; page 13, ©Christina Richards/
Shutterstock, Inc.; page 15, ©iStockphoto.com/duckycards; page 17, ©Kathy deWitt/Alamy;
page 19, ©sunsetman/Shutterstock, Inc.; page 21, ©Wolfephoto/Dreamstime.com

LIBRARY OF CONGRESS CATALOGING-IN-PUBLICATION DATA
Capici, Gaetano, 1985-
  What does it do? Cement mixer/by Gaetano Capici.
    p. cm.—(Community connections)
  Includes bibliographical references and index.
  ISBN-13: 978-1-60279-973-8 (lib. bdg.)
  ISBN-10: 1-60279-973-3 (lib. bdg.)
  1. Concrete mixers—Juvenile literature. I. Title. II. Title: Cement mixer. III. Series.
  TA439.C34 2011
  624.1'833—dc22   2010023581

Cherry Lake Publishing would like to acknowledge the
work of The Partnership for 21st Century Skills. Please
visit www.21stcenturyskills.org for more information.

Printed in the United States of America
Corporate Graphics Inc.
January 2011
CLSP08

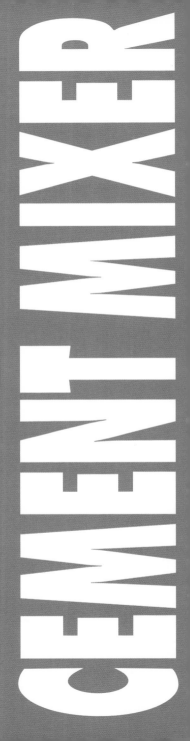

CONTENTS

WHAT DOES IT DO?

WHAT IS CONCRETE?

What is strong, hard, and used in building **projects**? Hint: You may see it every day. Can you guess? It is **concrete**!

Concrete is an important **building material**. It is used to make roads and sidewalks. It can be used in bridges and walls, too.

Can you see the concrete in this bridge?

Cement is a special gray powder. It is used to make concrete. Tiny stones, sand, and water are added, too.

At first, concrete is wet. Wet concrete is soft. It becomes hard and strong as it dries. Steel bars are sometimes added to the concrete. The bars make the concrete stronger.

This concrete will be spread over the steel bars.

Look around on your way to school. Keep an eye out for **structures** made with concrete. Do you spot any? How about sidewalks? Where else do you see concrete? Did you find more places than you expected?

MIXING IT UP

Cement mixers are important tools. They mix concrete and bring it to **construction sites**. Cement mixers are parts of special trucks. These trucks have large **drums**. The concrete is mixed in the drum. How? There is a special blade inside the drum. The drum turns one way. While it turns, the blade stirs the concrete.

The drum of this cement mixer is yellow with an orange stripe.

AT THE SITE

The drum turns as the mixer truck heads to a site. What happens when the driver reaches the site?

He backs the truck up to where concrete is needed. Workers set up a special slide called a **chute**. It is found at the back of the truck. Wet concrete will travel down the chute.

The chute directs the wet concrete to the right spot.

Remember how the drum turns to mix the concrete? It turns the opposite way when it is time to pour the concrete. The blade forces the concrete out of the drum. Down the chute it goes!

Concrete pours down the chute to where it is needed.

THINK!

Time is important when working with wet concrete. Workers must do the job quickly. Why do you think that is? Think about what happens to wet concrete after it is poured. How does it change?

13

Workers move the chute to spots that need concrete. This helps spread the concrete evenly.

Workers also smooth out the poured concrete by hand. Special tools help them do this.

Workers have to be careful not to step in the concrete after they smooth it out!

CREATE!

Cement mixers are big, heavy machines. Workers must stay safe. They must be careful when using moving parts such as chutes. Write down three ways to stay safe when using cement mixers. Ask an adult if you need help coming up with ideas.

What happens after the concrete is poured? The chute is folded back up. Then the cement mixer moves on to the next site.

The cement mixer is cleaned between jobs. It is rinsed with water. Workers remove any extra concrete. They try to do this before the concrete hardens on any machine parts.

It is important to keep the cement mixer clean.

IMPORTANT HELPERS

Imagine mixing a thick cake batter with a spoon. Picture mixing enough batter to make a cake as big as a sidewalk. You would be very tired!

Cement mixers help us in many ways. They save time and effort by mixing large amounts of concrete.

Not all cement mixers are parts of trucks. Small mixers are good for small jobs.

Think of cement mixers the next time you pass a bridge. Think of them when you see a **highway**. Cement mixers played a part in building these structures.

Look around the next time you spot a construction site. Are there any cement mixers? They are great machines. Now you know what they do!

You can spot cement mixers at many construction sites.

GLOSSARY

building material (BIL-ding muh-TIHR-ee-uhl) something used to build, such as brick or lumber

cement (suh-MENT) a powder that becomes hard when mixed with water and allowed to dry

chute (SHOOT) a tilted passage used to move things from one spot to another

concrete (KON-kreet) a special mix of sand, cement, water, and tiny stones

construction sites (kuhn-STRUHK-shuhn SITESS) areas where something is being built

drums (DRUHMZ) containers or machine parts that have round shapes

highway (HYE-way) a main road on which people can drive at high speeds

projects (PROJ-ektss) tasks that require a lot of work and planning

structures (STRUHK-churz) things that have been built

FIND OUT MORE

BOOKS

Addison, D. R. *Cement Mixers at Work*. New York: PowerKids Press, 2009.

Gilbert, Sara. *Concrete Mixers*. Mankato, MN: Creative Education, 2009.

WEB SITES

PBS—Building Big: Materials Lab
www.pbs.org/wgbh/buildingbig/lab/materials.html
See what happens when force is applied to concrete and other materials.

TLC—Natural Concrete Sculpture for Kids
tlc.howstuffworks.com/family/nature-craft-activities-for-kids6.htm
Mix homemade "concrete" and make fun craft projects.

INDEX

ABOUT THE AUTHOR

Gaetano Capici
graduated from
DePaul University
with bachelor's
degrees in English
and Spanish. He lives
near Chicago, Illinois.

24